Beyond Betrayal: Understanding and Healing from Infidelity

C. P. Kumar
Reiki Healer
Roorkee - 247667, India

Disclaimer

While every effort has been made to ensure the accuracy and completeness of the content in this book, the author cannot guarantee that the information contained herein is error-free, up-to-date, or suitable for every individual circumstance.

The author shall not be held liable or responsible for any errors or omissions in the content of the book, nor for any damages, or losses that may arise from any actions taken based upon the suggestions or contents presented in the book.

Readers are advised to use their own judgment and discretion in applying the information provided in this book, and to consult with qualified professionals before taking any action based on the contents of this book. The author disclaims any and all liability or responsibility for any actions taken or not taken based on the information contained in this book.

DEDICATION

To all those who have experienced the pain of betrayal,
May this book be a guiding light on your path to healing and understanding.

To the ones who have been hurt, feeling the shattering of trust,
May these words offer solace, strength, and hope as you navigate the aftermath.

To the ones who have strayed, seeking solace or escape,
May this knowledge bring awareness, insight, and the opportunity for growth.

To the couples who strive to rebuild, holding onto love amidst the wreckage,
May the wisdom within these pages provide guidance and inspiration as you forge a new path together.

To those who seek to prevent infidelity, fostering healthy relationships,
May this book offer insights, tools, and strategies to fortify the bonds of love and commitment.

This dedication is a testament to the resilience of the human spirit,
And a tribute to the enduring power of forgiveness, understanding, and personal transformation.

With deep empathy and unwavering compassion,
This book is dedicated to all those touched by the profound journey of "Beyond Betrayal: Understanding and Healing from Infidelity."

C. P. Kumar

CONTENTS

PREFACE

In the depths of human connection, where trust and vulnerability intertwine, lies a haunting reality that has plagued relationships throughout history: infidelity. The betrayal of a partner's faith, whether through physical or emotional trespasses, shatters the very foundations upon which love and commitment are built. It leaves wounds that run deep, casting doubt on the essence of our bonds and challenging the fabric of our identities.

"Beyond Betrayal: Understanding and Healing from Infidelity" delves into this complex and painful realm, aiming to shed light on the intricacies of infidelity and provide a roadmap for those navigating its treacherous terrain. Within these pages, we embark on a journey of exploration, compassion, and ultimately, healing.

The chapters that follow guide us through a comprehensive examination of the multifaceted nature of infidelity. We begin by setting the stage, unraveling the definitions and prevalence of extra-marital affairs while also exploring their historical and cultural dimensions. Through understanding the roots of infidelity, we lay the groundwork for empathy and comprehension.

Next, we dive into the various types of infidelity, unraveling the spectrum that encompasses emotional affairs, physical betrayals, cyber infidelity, and everything in between. By examining the motives, temptations, and opportunities that fuel these transgressions, we gain insights into the complexities that drive individuals to seek solace or excitement beyond their committed relationships.

Societal and cultural factors come under scrutiny as we explore the ways in which norms, attitudes, and media influence our perceptions of fidelity. We examine how these external forces shape our understandings of infidelity, offering a lens through which we can reflect on our own beliefs and judgments.

Turning inward, we delve into the psychological motivations that underlie infidelity. Unmet needs, attachment styles, and the quest for validation all intertwine with the human psyche, shedding light on the intricate dance between desire, dissatisfaction, and the choices we make within our relationships.

Communication and relationship dynamics take center stage as we explore the crucial role they play in the emergence and escalation of infidelity. The lack of emotional connection, power imbalances, and recurring patterns become key areas of investigation, providing invaluable insights for those seeking to prevent or heal from betrayals.

Sexuality and intimacy, cornerstones of romantic relationships, receive dedicated attention. We examine how sexual dissatisfaction and the pursuit of alternative arrangements contribute to the web of infidelity, while also delving into the distinctions between emotional and physical intimacy.

Gender perspectives further enrich our understanding as we confront societal expectations, stereotypes, and the unique experiences of men and women in the realm of infidelity. Recognizing the complex interplay of gender roles and motivations allows for a deeper comprehension of the impacts and challenges faced by individuals of different genders.

With empathy and compassion, we explore infidelity as a coping mechanism, addressing the ways in which stress, trauma, and personal struggles can lead to the seeking of solace through affairs. By acknowledging these underlying factors, we foster a more comprehensive understanding of infidelity's roots.

In the digital age, the internet emerges as a catalyst, facilitating connections and encounters that were once confined to physical spaces. We navigate the realm of online platforms, affair websites, and cyber infidelity, dissecting the allure, anonymity, and profound impact they have on relationships.

Emotional affair dynamics are brought to light, illuminating the slippery slope from friendship to emotional infidelity. The deep bonds formed and betrayed, the consequences of emotional unfaithfulness, and the importance of emotional fidelity itself become focal points of exploration.

Discovering an affair inflicts a heavy toll, and we delve into the emotional and psychological responses that reverberate through the betrayed partner. Confrontation, disclosure, and the aftermath become crucial milestones on the path to healing, with coping strategies and support systems offering a lifeline during this tumultuous journey.

The possibility of repairing a relationship post-infidelity is a question that weighs heavily on the hearts of many. We delve into the complexities, examining the role of therapy, professional guidance, and the factors that contribute to successful reconciliation. Through resilience and hope, we illuminate the possibility of rebuilding trust and finding a new path forward.

Consequences and repercussions reverberate not only within the core relationship but also in the lives of children and extended family. We navigate the emotional and psychological effects on both parties, while also examining the legal aspects and potential ramifications that arise from the aftermath of infidelity.

Cultural responses and perspectives on infidelity take us on a global journey, highlighting the variations in how different cultures approach and understand betrayal. Religious views, moral dilemmas, and cross-cultural differences in forgiveness and reconciliation further enrich our understanding of this universal yet culturally nuanced phenomenon.

As we reach the closing chapters, the focus shifts toward healing and moving forward. We explore the role of individual and couple's therapy in the recovery process, along with the vital tasks of rebuilding self-esteem and trust. Through personal growth and newfound insights, we unveil the growth opportunities that can emerge from the ashes of an affair.

Prevention becomes paramount as we conclude this journey, addressing the importance of nurturing healthy relationships, effective communication, and strategies to fortify emotional bonds. By fostering resilience and creating environments conducive to trust and connection, we strive to prevent the wounds of infidelity from ever surfacing.

Finally, we expand our horizons, exploring the realm of relationships beyond infidelity. Open relationships, consensual non-monogamy, and evolving models challenge traditional notions of monogamy, inviting us to reconsider and redefine the landscape of love and commitment.

"Beyond Betrayal: Understanding and Healing from Infidelity" is a tapestry woven with compassion, research, and real-life experiences. It is a guidebook for those grappling with the aftermath of infidelity, offering insights and tools for healing wounds, rebuilding trust, and reimagining relationships. It is an invitation to a deeper understanding of ourselves and others, as we navigate the complex terrain of love, betrayal, and ultimately, transformation.

C. P. Kumar

Reiki Healer

Former Scientist 'G', National Institute of Hydrology
Roorkee - 247667, India
E-mail: cpkumar@yahoo.com
Web: https://www.angelfire.com/nh/cpkumar/virgo.html

Introduction

Infidelity, the breach of trust within a committed relationship, is a deeply painful and complex phenomenon that has been a part of human history since time immemorial. It carries profound emotional consequences for all parties involved and can leave lasting scars on the fabric of relationships. In "Beyond Betrayal: Understanding and Healing from Infidelity," we embark on a journey to explore the intricate layers of infidelity, seeking to provide insights and guidance for those who have experienced its devastating effects. In this introductory chapter, we will define extra-marital affairs, examine their prevalence in society, and delve into the historical and cultural perspectives that shape our understanding of infidelity.

Defining extra-marital affairs and their prevalence

To comprehend the true essence of infidelity, it is essential to establish a clear definition. Extra-marital affairs encompass any form of betrayal that involves one or both partners engaging in emotional or physical connections outside the committed relationship. This can range from clandestine emotional bonds to secret sexual encounters. By acknowledging the vast spectrum of infidelity, we can begin to understand its multifaceted nature and the diverse ways it manifests within relationships.

The prevalence of infidelity is a topic that both intrigues and alarms us. While obtaining precise statistics on the occurrence of extra-marital affairs is challenging due to the secretive nature of such acts, studies and surveys provide us with valuable insights. Research suggests that infidelity is more common than we might anticipate, with prevalence rates varying across cultures, age groups, and relationship types. Acknowledging the prevalence of infidelity helps us recognize that we are not alone in our experiences, fostering a sense of empathy and shared understanding.

Historical and cultural perspectives on infidelity

Infidelity is not a modern phenomenon but rather an intrinsic part of human history. Throughout the ages, relationships have grappled with the complexities of fidelity, and societies have grappled with how to address it. Historical perspectives on infidelity have been influenced by various factors, including cultural norms, religious beliefs, and societal structures.

In ancient civilizations, such as ancient Greece and Rome, infidelity was often tolerated among men, while women were held to stricter standards of fidelity. The concept of arranged marriages and political alliances further complicated notions of fidelity, as marriages were often pragmatic unions rather than expressions of love and desire. In contrast, some indigenous cultures, such as certain Native American tribes, had more flexible views on relationships and allowed for multiple partners within the context of consensual non-monogamy.

Cultural perspectives on infidelity continue to shape our understanding in contemporary society. Attitudes towards infidelity can differ greatly, ranging from condemnation and stigmatization to more nuanced perspectives that acknowledge the complexity of human relationships. Cultural factors, such as religious beliefs, social expectations, and gender roles, play a significant role in influencing these attitudes.

Religious doctrines and moral codes also contribute to the understanding of infidelity. Many religious traditions consider infidelity to be a grave sin or a violation of sacred vows. These religious perspectives can significantly impact individuals' perceptions of infidelity and shape the guidance they receive in navigating its aftermath.

Conclusion

In this introductory chapter, we have embarked on a journey into the realm of infidelity. We have defined extra-marital affairs, recognizing the spectrum of emotional and physical betrayals that occur within relationships. By understanding the prevalence of infidelity, we acknowledge the ubiquity of this phenomenon, bringing solace to those who have experienced its devastating effects.

Furthermore, we have explored historical and cultural perspectives on infidelity, recognizing the diverse ways in which societies have grappled with this complex issue throughout time. These perspectives provide a valuable context for understanding the evolution of societal norms and expectations surrounding fidelity.

As we continue our exploration in the subsequent chapters of "Beyond Betrayal: Understanding and Healing from Infidelity," we will delve deeper into the different types of infidelity, societal and cultural influences, psychological motivations, communication dynamics, and the journey towards healing and prevention. By broadening our understanding and offering guidance, we hope to provide a compass for those navigating the turbulent waters of infidelity, leading them towards a path of understanding, healing, and the possibility of rebuilding trust and love in their relationships.

Introduction

Infidelity is not a one-size-fits-all concept. It manifests in various forms, each carrying its unique dynamics, consequences, and emotional impact. In this chapter of "Beyond Betrayal: Understanding and Healing from Infidelity," we delve into the spectrum of infidelity, exploring the distinctions between emotional affairs and physical affairs, one-time flings and long-term affairs, and the emerging realm of cyber infidelity. By understanding the nuances of each type, we can gain insights into the complexities of infidelity and its profound effects on relationships.

Emotional affairs vs. physical affairs

Infidelity extends beyond the physical realm, encompassing emotional connections that breach the boundaries of a committed relationship. Emotional affairs involve a deep emotional bond with someone other than one's partner, often involving intense feelings of intimacy, companionship, and romantic attraction. Unlike physical affairs, emotional infidelity may not involve sexual encounters but can be just as devastating to the betrayed partner.

Physical affairs, on the other hand, involve sexual encounters outside the committed relationship. They can range from one-time flings, fueled by momentary desires or opportunities, to long-term affairs characterized by ongoing clandestine relationships. Physical affairs often carry a different set of challenges, as they directly breach the boundaries of sexual exclusivity and can be perceived as a deeper betrayal.

One-time flings vs. long-term affairs

One-time flings refer to brief, spontaneous encounters that occur outside the confines of a committed relationship. These encounters may be driven by various factors, such as curiosity, novelty, or dissatisfaction within the current relationship. While one-time flings may not involve emotional attachments, they can still inflict significant pain and damage to the primary relationship.

In contrast, long-term affairs involve ongoing, often hidden relationships with someone other than one's partner. These affairs can develop over time, marked by sustained emotional and sexual involvement. Long-term affairs often carry a greater degree of emotional entanglement and can pose a formidable threat to the stability and trust within the committed relationship.

Cyber infidelity and the impact of technology

In today's digital age, infidelity has taken on new dimensions with the rise of cyber infidelity. This form of betrayal encompasses online interactions, virtual connections, and engagements through various technological platforms. Dating apps, social media, and online forums have become breeding grounds for emotional and sexual connections outside established relationships.

Cyber infidelity offers a unique set of challenges, as it blurs the boundaries between the virtual and physical worlds. The allure of anonymity, convenience, and the ability to seek connections discreetly can make online platforms particularly tempting for those seeking excitement or emotional fulfillment outside their committed relationships. The impact of technology on infidelity is profound, reshaping the landscape of trust and intimacy within relationships.

Conclusion

In this chapter, we have explored the spectrum of infidelity, recognizing that it encompasses more than just physical encounters. Emotional affairs and physical affairs carry distinct dynamics and emotional consequences, both capable of causing significant harm to the committed relationship. One-time flings and long-term affairs represent different durations and levels of emotional involvement, with each posing unique challenges to the betrayed partner.

Furthermore, we have examined the emergence of cyber infidelity and its impact on relationships. The rise of technology has facilitated virtual connections and expanded the possibilities for infidelity, creating new avenues for emotional and sexual betrayal.

Understanding the spectrum of infidelity allows us to grasp the complexities and ramifications that arise when boundaries are breached within committed relationships. By acknowledging these distinctions, we can provide guidance and insights to those grappling with the aftermath of infidelity, offering a compass for understanding, healing, and rebuilding trust in the wake of betrayal. As we proceed through the subsequent chapters of "Beyond Betrayal: Understanding and Healing from Infidelity," we will continue to explore the multifaceted aspects of infidelity, shedding light on societal influences, psychological motivations, communication dynamics, and the journey towards healing and prevention.

Introduction

Infidelity is not only a deeply personal experience but also one that is influenced by societal and cultural factors. Our understanding of fidelity and the consequences associated with its breach are not formed in isolation but are shaped by the norms, values, and beliefs prevalent in our society. In this chapter of "Beyond Betrayal: Understanding and Healing from Infidelity," we delve into the societal and cultural factors that influence our perceptions of infidelity. We explore how societal norms shape our understanding of fidelity, the variations in attitudes towards infidelity across cultures, and the impact of media and popular culture on our perceptions of faithfulness.

How societal norms influence perceptions of fidelity

Societal norms act as a framework within which our behaviors and expectations are constructed. They define what is deemed acceptable or unacceptable within a given society. In the realm of relationships, societal norms play a pivotal role in shaping our perceptions of fidelity. These norms establish the boundaries of commitment, faithfulness, and loyalty within partnerships.

Cultural norms, religious beliefs, and legal frameworks contribute to the development of societal norms surrounding infidelity. For example, cultures that prioritize collectivism and emphasize community harmony may view infidelity as not only a betrayal of the individual partner but also a disruption of societal stability. In contrast, cultures that prioritize individual autonomy and personal happiness may place greater emphasis on personal fulfillment, potentially impacting perceptions of fidelity.

Cultural variations in attitudes towards infidelity

Attitudes towards infidelity vary significantly across different cultures and societies. What may be considered an egregious transgression in one culture could be viewed with greater tolerance or even acceptance in another. Cultural factors such as religion, historical traditions, and social structures influence these attitudes.

For instance, cultures with a strong religious influence may view infidelity as a moral violation, often equating it with sin or immorality. In contrast, cultures with a more permissive view of sexuality and relationships may adopt a more open-minded stance towards non-monogamy or consensual non-monogamy.

It is essential to acknowledge these cultural variations to avoid imposing a single, universal standard for fidelity. Recognizing and respecting diverse cultural perspectives allows for a more comprehensive understanding of the complexities surrounding infidelity and the different ways in which individuals and societies navigate these challenges.

The impact of media and popular culture on infidelity

Media, including movies, television shows, and music, often play a significant role in shaping societal perceptions and influencing our understanding of relationships. Popular culture can both reflect and perpetuate certain narratives surrounding infidelity. Portrayals of affairs in the media can range from glamorizing and normalizing infidelity to highlighting the devastating consequences it can have on individuals and relationships.

Media depictions often shape societal discourse and influence our collective consciousness. They can create unrealistic expectations of relationships, normalize infidelity as an inherent part of human nature, or raise awareness about the emotional turmoil it can cause. Therefore, media and popular culture have the power to shape public opinion and impact the ways in which individuals perceive and respond to infidelity.

Conclusion

Societal and cultural factors significantly influence our perceptions of infidelity. Societal norms establish the boundaries and expectations of fidelity within relationships, shaping our understanding of commitment and loyalty. Cultural variations contribute to diverse attitudes towards infidelity, reflecting differing values, religious beliefs, and historical traditions. Additionally, media and popular culture play a substantial role in shaping societal narratives surrounding infidelity, influencing our collective understanding and responses to these issues.

Understanding the influence of societal and cultural factors is crucial in developing a nuanced perspective on infidelity. By recognizing and respecting diverse viewpoints, we can cultivate empathy, tolerance, and a deeper understanding of the complexities surrounding infidelity. As we progress through the subsequent chapters of "Beyond Betrayal: Understanding and Healing from Infidelity," we will continue to explore psychological motivations, communication dynamics, healing processes, and prevention strategies, incorporating the interplay of societal and cultural factors into our exploration of infidelity.

Introduction

Infidelity is not solely a matter of external circumstances or temptations but is deeply rooted in psychological motivations that drive individuals to breach the boundaries of committed relationships. In this chapter of "Beyond Betrayal: Understanding and Healing from Infidelity," we delve into the psychological underpinnings of infidelity. We explore how unmet needs and desires within relationships, attachment styles, and self-esteem influence the likelihood of infidelity. By understanding these psychological motivations, we can gain insights into the complex inner dynamics that contribute to betrayal and seek pathways towards healing and prevention.

Unmet needs and desires within relationships

Within a committed relationship, individuals have a multitude of needs and desires that contribute to their overall well-being and sense of fulfillment. When these needs are unmet or suppressed, it can create a breeding ground for discontent and vulnerability to infidelity. Emotional intimacy, sexual satisfaction, companionship, validation, and personal growth are examples of essential needs that, when neglected, can leave individuals susceptible to seeking fulfillment outside the relationship.

Unfulfilled needs and desires can stem from various factors, including communication breakdowns, relational imbalances, or unresolved conflicts. When individuals feel chronically dissatisfied or disconnected from their partners, they may be compelled to seek validation, emotional intimacy, or excitement elsewhere.

Attachment styles and their influence on infidelity

Attachment styles, which are formed early in life through interactions with primary caregivers, significantly impact the quality and dynamics of adult relationships. Insecure attachment styles, such as anxious or avoidant attachment, can increase the likelihood of infidelity.

Individuals with anxious attachment styles often exhibit a deep fear of abandonment and seek constant reassurance and validation. They may be more prone to seeking emotional connections outside the primary relationship as a means of soothing their insecurities and obtaining the attention they crave.

On the other hand, individuals with avoidant attachment styles tend to be more emotionally distant and reluctant to fully engage in intimate relationships. They may be more inclined to seek external validation or physical encounters to avoid the vulnerability and emotional closeness associated with committed relationships.

Understanding the influence of attachment styles can provide valuable insights into the underlying psychological motivations that contribute to infidelity. It underscores the importance of addressing attachment wounds and fostering secure and healthy emotional connections within relationships.

The role of self-esteem and validation-seeking behavior

Self-esteem plays a critical role in how individuals perceive themselves and seek validation from others. Individuals with low self-esteem may be more vulnerable to seeking external validation and attention, which can increase the likelihood of engaging in infidelity.

Seeking validation through external sources, such as engaging in flirtatious behaviors or seeking affirmation from other potential partners, can provide a temporary boost to one's self-esteem. However, this validation-seeking behavior can lead individuals down a treacherous path, risking the stability of their committed relationship.

Additionally, individuals with low self-esteem may struggle with feelings of unworthiness or inadequacy within the relationship. These insecurities can drive them to seek affirmation and validation outside the relationship, believing that it will fill the void they experience within themselves.

Conclusion

The motivations behind infidelity extend far beyond external temptations or circumstances. Unmet needs and desires within relationships, attachment styles, and self-esteem all play significant roles in shaping the likelihood of infidelity. By understanding these psychological motivations, we can gain insights into the intricate inner dynamics that contribute to betrayal.

Recognizing the importance of addressing unmet needs and desires within relationships allows for a more proactive approach to preventing infidelity. Nurturing open communication, fostering emotional and sexual satisfaction, and creating an environment of trust and security are vital components of maintaining a healthy, fulfilling relationship.

Moreover, understanding attachment styles and their influence on infidelity highlights the need for self-awareness and personal growth. By recognizing and addressing insecurities and attachment wounds, individuals can work towards developing secure attachment styles and fostering healthier, more satisfying relationships.

As we progress through the subsequent chapters of "Beyond Betrayal: Understanding and Healing from Infidelity," we will continue to explore communication dynamics, healing processes, and prevention strategies, incorporating the insights gained from understanding the psychological motivations behind infidelity.

Introduction

Effective communication is the lifeblood of any healthy and thriving relationship. It serves as a foundation for trust, understanding, and emotional intimacy. However, when communication breaks down or becomes ineffective, relationships can become vulnerable to infidelity. In this chapter of "Beyond Betrayal: Understanding and Healing from Infidelity," we delve into the crucial role of communication in relationships. We explore the detrimental effects of a lack of communication and emotional disconnection, the impact of power imbalances and relational dissatisfaction, and the relationship patterns that contribute to infidelity. By understanding these dynamics, we can navigate the complexities of communication and work towards preventing infidelity.

Lack of communication and emotional disconnection

Communication serves as a bridge between partners, enabling them to express their needs, desires, concerns, and emotions. When communication becomes strained or absent, couples may experience a growing emotional distance and a lack of connection. This breakdown in communication can create an environment conducive to infidelity.

A lack of communication often leads to misunderstandings, unaddressed issues, and unmet needs within the relationship. Partners may feel unheard, dismissed, or emotionally neglected, leading to a sense of dissatisfaction and frustration. This emotional disconnection can leave individuals vulnerable to seeking emotional fulfillment or validation outside the relationship.

Cultivating open and honest communication is essential for fostering emotional intimacy and maintaining a strong bond. It requires active listening, empathy, and a willingness to engage in difficult conversations. By actively communicating and addressing issues as they arise, couples can work towards building a solid foundation of trust and connection, reducing the risk of infidelity.

Power imbalances and relational dissatisfaction

Power imbalances within relationships can significantly impact communication dynamics and contribute to the risk of infidelity. When one partner holds more power or control over decision-making, emotions, or resources, it can create an environment of dissatisfaction and resentment.

Relational dissatisfaction often arises from feelings of inequality, lack of autonomy, or a sense of being taken for granted. These feelings can erode the emotional connection between partners, making individuals more susceptible to seeking validation, emotional intimacy, or a sense of empowerment outside the relationship.

Addressing power imbalances requires a commitment to equality, mutual respect, and shared decision-making. By fostering an environment where both partners have a voice and agency, couples can strengthen their bond and reduce the vulnerability to infidelity.

Relationship patterns that contribute to infidelity

Unhealthy relationship patterns can contribute to the likelihood of infidelity. Patterns such as chronic conflict, emotional neglect, or a pattern of seeking external validation can create an atmosphere of dissatisfaction and disconnection.

Chronic conflict can create a hostile environment within the relationship, leading individuals to seek emotional solace or escape through infidelity. Emotional neglect, where one or both partners fail to meet each other's emotional needs, can leave individuals vulnerable to seeking emotional connections elsewhere. Additionally, individuals who have a pattern of seeking external validation may be more prone to seeking affirmation, attention, or excitement outside the relationship.

Recognizing and addressing unhealthy relationship patterns is crucial for preventing infidelity. Couples can benefit from couples therapy, individual therapy, or relationship education programs to learn healthier communication skills, address underlying issues, and establish healthier patterns of interaction.

Conclusion

Communication is the cornerstone of a healthy and resilient relationship, serving as a vital tool for fostering emotional intimacy, understanding, and trust. A lack of communication and emotional disconnection can pave the way for infidelity, as individuals seek fulfillment outside the relationship. Power imbalances and relational dissatisfaction further increase the vulnerability to betrayal.

To prevent infidelity, couples must prioritize open and honest communication, actively listen to one another, and address issues as they arise. Creating an environment of equality, respect, and shared decision-making can help reduce the risk of power imbalances. Additionally, identifying and addressing unhealthy relationship patterns can strengthen the bond between partners and reduce the likelihood of seeking external connections.

As we progress through the subsequent chapters of "Beyond Betrayal: Understanding and Healing from Infidelity," we will continue to explore healing processes, prevention strategies, and the exploration of alternative relationship models. By nurturing communication and understanding relationship dynamics, individuals can foster strong, fulfilling connections that withstand the challenges and temptations that may arise in the context of infidelity.

Introduction

In the realm of relationships, temptations and opportunities can arise unexpectedly, posing significant challenges to the commitment and loyalty of individuals. In this chapter of "Beyond Betrayal: Understanding and Healing from Infidelity," we delve into the complex landscape of temptations and opportunities that can lead to infidelity. We explore the dynamics of workplace affairs and office romances, the role of social media and online platforms as catalysts for connection, and the influence of proximity and familiarity in fostering illicit relationships. By understanding these factors, we can navigate the pathways to infidelity and work towards preserving the sanctity of committed partnerships.

Workplace affairs and office romances

The workplace is a breeding ground for both professional growth and potential complications within relationships. With long hours, shared goals, and close proximity, individuals may develop emotional connections or engage in affairs with colleagues.

Workplace affairs can be particularly enticing, as they often involve a combination of emotional support, intellectual stimulation, and shared experiences. The emotional intimacy formed through collaboration and daily interactions can blur the boundaries of professional and personal relationships, creating an environment conducive to infidelity.

Office romances, on the other hand, involve consensual relationships between colleagues. While some office romances flourish and transition into committed partnerships, others may become sources of conflict and betrayal within existing relationships.

Navigating workplace dynamics and establishing clear boundaries is crucial for preventing workplace affairs and mitigating the risks associated with office romances. Open communication with one's partner, maintaining professional boundaries, and fostering a supportive and inclusive work environment can help individuals navigate the complexities of workplace relationships and reduce the likelihood of infidelity.

Social media and online platforms as catalysts

The advent of social media and online platforms has significantly transformed the landscape of relationships and introduced new avenues for connection. These platforms offer opportunities for individuals to expand their social networks, reconnect with past acquaintances, and engage in virtual interactions that can lead to emotional or physical infidelity.

Social media can provide a sense of anonymity, making it easier for individuals to engage in secretive or illicit connections. The allure of virtual connections, the potential for emotional validation, and the access to a wide range of potential partners can be tempting for those who feel dissatisfied or unfulfilled in their current relationships.

Online platforms, such as dating websites or affair-specific websites, further contribute to the proliferation of infidelity. These platforms create opportunities for individuals to seek extramarital affairs or engage in casual encounters, often under the guise of anonymity or discretion.

It is essential to approach social media and online platforms with caution and open communication within relationships. Establishing guidelines, discussing boundaries, and maintaining transparency can help mitigate the risks associated with these platforms and maintain the trust and commitment within a partnership.

The influence of proximity and familiarity

Proximity and familiarity can significantly impact the likelihood of infidelity. When individuals are consistently exposed to others who share common interests, engage in daily interactions, or experience similar life circumstances, the potential for emotional or physical connections may increase.

Proximity can create opportunities for individuals to develop emotional bonds and establish connections beyond their existing relationships. Shared experiences, mutual support, and the absence of physical distance can foster a sense of intimacy and emotional connection that can be challenging to resist.

Familiarity, whether through longstanding friendships or close social circles, can also contribute to the risk of infidelity. Familiarity may breed a sense of comfort and ease, blurring the boundaries of what is acceptable within a committed relationship.

Maintaining awareness of the impact of proximity and familiarity is crucial for individuals in committed relationships. Setting boundaries, engaging in open communication, and actively investing in the emotional and physical connection with one's partner can help individuals navigate the potential temptations and risks associated with proximity and familiarity.

Conclusion

Temptations and opportunities are ever-present in the realm of relationships, posing challenges to the commitment and loyalty of individuals. Workplace affairs and office romances can blur professional and personal boundaries, requiring individuals to establish clear guidelines and maintain open communication. Social media and online platforms offer new pathways for connection, necessitating caution, transparency, and adherence to agreed-upon boundaries. Proximity and familiarity can create emotional bonds and increase the risk of infidelity, emphasizing the need for individuals to prioritize the emotional and physical connection within their committed relationships.

By understanding and navigating the dynamics of temptations and opportunities, individuals can work towards preserving the integrity of their partnerships. As we progress through the subsequent chapters of "Beyond Betrayal: Understanding and Healing from Infidelity," we will continue to explore healing processes, prevention strategies, and the exploration of alternative relationship models, incorporating the insights gained from understanding the pathways to infidelity.

Introduction

Intimacy and sexuality are fundamental aspects of human relationships, playing a crucial role in the satisfaction and fulfillment of individuals within committed partnerships. However, when these needs are unmet or neglected, they can contribute to the vulnerability of infidelity. In this chapter of "Beyond Betrayal: Understanding and Healing from Infidelity," we delve into the intricate dynamics of intimacy and sexuality. We explore the impact of sexual dissatisfaction on infidelity, the distinction between emotional intimacy and physical intimacy, and the exploration of alternative sexual arrangements. By understanding these factors, individuals can navigate the complexities of intimacy and sexuality, fostering healthy connections and preventing the erosion of trust and commitment.

Impact of sexual dissatisfaction on infidelity

Sexual satisfaction is an essential component of a fulfilling relationship, contributing to the emotional, physical, and psychological well-being of individuals. When sexual needs and desires are not adequately met within a partnership, it can create a sense of frustration, resentment, and disconnection.

Sexual dissatisfaction can stem from various factors, including differences in libido, mismatched sexual preferences, or unresolved sexual issues. When individuals feel consistently dissatisfied or unfulfilled in their sexual experiences, they may become vulnerable to seeking sexual gratification outside the relationship, leading to infidelity.

Open and honest communication about sexual needs and desires is crucial for addressing and resolving sexual dissatisfaction within a partnership. By creating a safe space for discussing preferences, exploring new experiences, and seeking professional guidance if needed, couples can work towards fostering sexual satisfaction and reducing the risk of infidelity.

Emotional intimacy vs. physical intimacy

Intimacy encompasses both emotional and physical aspects of a relationship. Emotional intimacy involves the deep connection, trust, and vulnerability shared between partners, while physical intimacy refers to the sexual and physical expressions of affection.

Emotional intimacy is the foundation upon which a strong and resilient relationship is built. It involves open communication, active listening, empathy, and the sharing of hopes, fears, and dreams. Emotional intimacy fosters a sense of connection and closeness that goes beyond physical interactions, deepening the bond between partners.

Physical intimacy, on the other hand, encompasses sexual experiences and physical expressions of affection. It plays a crucial role in the physical and emotional satisfaction of individuals within a relationship. Physical intimacy can deepen emotional connection, enhance trust, and reinforce the overall satisfaction and well-being of both partners.

Maintaining a balance between emotional and physical intimacy is vital for the health and longevity of a relationship. Both aspects contribute to the overall sense of fulfillment and connectedness. By nurturing emotional intimacy through open communication, trust-building exercises, and quality time spent together, couples can create a solid foundation for physical intimacy, reducing the risk of seeking fulfillment outside the relationship.

Exploring alternative sexual arrangements

For some individuals, the exploration of alternative sexual arrangements may be a means of addressing sexual dissatisfaction or fulfilling personal desires while maintaining the commitment to their primary partnership. These arrangements can include consensual non-monogamy, open relationships, or other forms of negotiated agreements.

Exploring alternative sexual arrangements requires open and honest communication, clear boundaries, and the consent of all parties involved. It is crucial for individuals to engage in self-reflection, consider their own comfort levels and motivations, and have ongoing discussions with their partners to ensure that these arrangements align with their values and relationship goals.

However, it is important to note that alternative sexual arrangements may not be suitable or desired by everyone. It is essential for couples to have open and honest conversations about their boundaries, expectations, and values before engaging in such arrangements. Each partnership is unique, and what works for one couple may not work for another.

Conclusion

Intimacy and sexuality are integral components of fulfilling and healthy relationships. Sexual dissatisfaction can create vulnerabilities that increase the risk of infidelity, highlighting the importance of open communication and addressing sexual needs within a partnership. Emotional intimacy and physical intimacy both contribute to the overall satisfaction and connectedness of individuals, requiring a balance and mutual investment. Exploring alternative sexual arrangements may be an option for some couples, but it is essential to approach such discussions with honesty, consent, and ongoing communication.

By understanding and nurturing the role of intimacy and sexuality, individuals can foster strong and resilient connections, reducing the likelihood of seeking fulfillment outside the relationship. As we progress through the subsequent chapters of "Beyond Betrayal: Understanding and Healing from Infidelity," we will continue to explore healing processes, prevention strategies, and the exploration of evolving relationship models, incorporating the insights gained from understanding the dynamics of intimacy and sexuality.

Introduction

Infidelity is a complex phenomenon that can affect individuals of all genders, but it is important to acknowledge that gender perspectives play a significant role in understanding the motivations behind infidelity and its impact on men and women. In this chapter of "Beyond Betrayal: Understanding and Healing from Infidelity," we delve into the intricacies of gender perspectives in relation to infidelity. We explore how stereotypes and societal expectations shape our understanding of fidelity, the gender differences in motivations for infidelity, and the unique impact that infidelity can have on men and women. By gaining insights into these gender dynamics, we can foster empathy, understanding, and healing in the aftermath of betrayal.

Stereotypes and societal expectations

Stereotypes and societal expectations surrounding gender and relationships have a profound influence on our understanding of fidelity. Society often expects men and women to adhere to different roles and behaviors within their relationships, which can create pressure and constraints.

Men are often stereotypically portrayed as having a stronger sexual drive and a greater need for variety in their sexual experiences. This stereotype can contribute to the perception that men are more prone to infidelity. On the other hand, women are sometimes portrayed as more emotionally driven, seeking emotional connection outside of their primary partnership. These gender stereotypes can oversimplify the complexities of human desires and motivations.

It is important to challenge and question these stereotypes to foster a more nuanced understanding of infidelity. Recognizing that individuals of all genders can experience a range of motivations for infidelity allows for a more compassionate and accurate assessment of the dynamics at play.

Gender differences in motivations for infidelity

While infidelity can occur regardless of gender, research suggests that men and women may have different motivations behind their extramarital involvement. Men may be more likely to engage in infidelity due to sexual novelty, a desire for sexual variety, or to enhance their sense of masculinity and validation. Women, on the other hand, may be more likely to engage in infidelity due to emotional dissatisfaction in their current relationship, seeking emotional intimacy, or as a response to unmet emotional needs.

However, it is important to note that these motivations are not universal or exclusive to any gender. Motivations for infidelity can vary greatly among individuals, and it is essential to approach each situation with an open mind and a willingness to understand the unique experiences and needs of the individuals involved.

The impact of infidelity on men and women

Infidelity can have profound emotional, psychological, and social impacts on both men and women. The experience of betrayal and the resulting emotional turmoil can lead to a range of reactions and consequences. Men and women may respond differently to infidelity due to societal expectations, gender roles, and individual differences in coping mechanisms.

Women may experience feelings of betrayal, loss, and questioning of their self-worth. They may also grapple with issues of trust and may have difficulty rebuilding the emotional connection with their partner after the breach of fidelity.

Men, on the other hand, may experience a sense of emasculation, loss of self-esteem, and questioning of their own desirability. They may also face societal judgment and stereotypes that compound their emotional distress.

It is important to approach the healing process with sensitivity and empathy, recognizing that the impact of infidelity can be deeply personal and unique to each individual, regardless of gender.

Conclusion

Gender perspectives play a significant role in understanding infidelity, as stereotypes and societal expectations shape our perceptions of fidelity and influence the motivations behind extramarital involvement. Recognizing and challenging these stereotypes allows for a more nuanced understanding of infidelity and encourages empathy and compassion in the aftermath of betrayal.

While there may be gender differences in motivations for infidelity, it is crucial to approach each situation with an open mind and recognize that motivations can vary greatly among individuals. Infidelity can have a profound impact on both men and women, and the healing process requires sensitivity, understanding, and a willingness to rebuild trust and emotional connection.

As we progress through the subsequent chapters of "Beyond Betrayal: Understanding and Healing from Infidelity," we will continue to explore healing processes, prevention strategies, and the exploration of cultural responses to infidelity, incorporating the insights gained from understanding the dynamics of gender perspectives.

Introduction

Infidelity is a deeply complex and multifaceted issue that can have devastating effects on relationships and individuals involved. In this chapter of "Beyond Betrayal: Understanding and Healing from Infidelity," we delve into the concept of infidelity as a coping mechanism. We explore how individuals may turn to extramarital affairs as a way of dealing with stress, trauma, and personal issues. We also examine the role of emotional escape and self-soothing through affairs, as well as how infidelity can manifest as a response to relationship dissatisfaction. By understanding these complexities, we can shed light on the underlying motivations and challenges faced by individuals who engage in infidelity and begin the healing process.

Dealing with stress, trauma, and personal issues

Life is full of challenges, and individuals may face various stressors, traumas, and personal issues that can take a toll on their well-being and relationships. Infidelity, in some cases, may be seen as a coping mechanism to alleviate the pain or escape from the difficulties they are facing.

Stressors such as work pressures, financial strain, or personal hardships can create emotional and psychological distress, leading individuals to seek solace or distraction outside their committed relationships. Similarly, individuals who have experienced trauma, such as the loss of a loved one or past abuse, may find it challenging to confront and process their pain, leading them to turn to extramarital affairs as a means of numbing or avoiding their emotions.

Understanding the underlying stressors, traumas, and personal issues that may contribute to infidelity is crucial for addressing the root causes and supporting individuals in finding healthier coping mechanisms.

Emotional escape and self-soothing through affairs

Infidelity can provide a temporary escape from the challenges and responsibilities of daily life, allowing individuals to experience moments of emotional connection, excitement, and validation. Engaging in an affair may serve as a way to fulfill unmet emotional needs, seek validation, or experience a sense of self-worth.

For some individuals, the affair partner becomes a source of emotional support and understanding that may be lacking in their primary relationship. This emotional escape can provide a temporary respite from the challenges faced within their committed partnership.

Furthermore, self-soothing through affairs may offer a sense of control or agency, allowing individuals to regain a sense of power or autonomy that they feel is lacking in their primary relationship. However, it is essential to recognize that this temporary escape and self-soothing are ultimately counterproductive, as they undermine the trust, commitment, and emotional well-being of all parties involved.

Infidelity as a response to relationship dissatisfaction

Infidelity can also manifest as a response to relationship dissatisfaction, where individuals may seek fulfillment of their unmet needs or desires outside their primary partnership. Relationship dissatisfaction can stem from various factors, including a lack of emotional connection, sexual dissatisfaction, or communication breakdown.

When individuals feel unfulfilled within their relationships, they may seek external sources of validation, excitement, or passion. Infidelity may be perceived as an opportunity to regain a sense of vitality and fulfillment that is absent in their current partnership.

Understanding and addressing the underlying issues contributing to relationship dissatisfaction is crucial for individuals seeking to repair and rebuild their committed relationships. It requires open communication, active listening, and a willingness to work together to address the unmet needs and desires within the partnership.

Conclusion

Infidelity as a coping mechanism is a complex phenomenon influenced by various stressors, traumas, and personal issues. It can serve as a temporary escape, self-soothing mechanism, or response to relationship dissatisfaction. However, it is essential to recognize that while infidelity may offer temporary relief, it ultimately exacerbates the pain, erodes trust, and poses significant challenges to the healing and rebuilding process.

Understanding the underlying motivations and challenges faced by individuals who engage in infidelity is a crucial step toward healing and growth. By addressing the root causes of infidelity, individuals can seek healthier coping mechanisms, address relationship issues, and work towards rebuilding trust, fostering emotional connection, and preventing further harm.

As we progress through the subsequent chapters of "Beyond Betrayal: Understanding and Healing from Infidelity," we will continue to explore healing processes, prevention strategies, and the exploration of alternative relationship models, incorporating the insights gained from understanding the complexities of infidelity as a coping mechanism.

Introduction

The advent of the internet has transformed the way we connect, communicate, and form relationships. While the internet offers numerous benefits, it has also given rise to new challenges and complexities, particularly in the realm of infidelity. In this chapter of "Beyond Betrayal: Understanding and Healing from Infidelity," we delve into the intricate relationship between the internet and infidelity. We explore the role of online dating platforms and affair websites, the allure of virtual connections facilitated by the anonymity factor, and the impact of cyber infidelity on relationships. By understanding these dynamics, individuals can navigate the digital landscape with greater awareness and take proactive steps towards healing and prevention.

Online dating platforms and affair websites

The proliferation of online dating platforms and affair websites has created new avenues for individuals to seek extramarital connections. These platforms offer a degree of convenience, anonymity, and access to a wider pool of potential partners. Individuals may be drawn to these platforms in search of novelty, excitement, or a sense of fulfillment that they perceive as lacking in their current relationships.

Online dating platforms cater to a range of relationship preferences, from casual encounters to long-term affairs. Affair websites specifically target individuals seeking discreet and secretive extramarital relationships. The ease of creating profiles, engaging in online interactions, and arranging in-person meetings has significantly altered the landscape of infidelity.

It is essential to recognize that while these platforms may facilitate connections, they also pose risks and challenges to individuals, relationships, and families. Understanding the motivations behind seeking connections through online platforms is crucial for addressing the root causes and developing healthier strategies for relationship fulfillment.

The anonymity factor and the allure of virtual connections

The internet provides a sense of anonymity that can be appealing to individuals seeking extramarital connections. The ability to create online personas or engage in virtual interactions can foster a false sense of security and freedom from consequences. This anonymity can embolden individuals to explore their desires and engage in behaviors they may not consider in offline settings.

Virtual connections may also provide a temporary escape from the challenges and responsibilities of real-life relationships. Online interactions can create a fantasy world where individuals can feel desired, validated, or understood. This allure of virtual connections can be particularly enticing to individuals who feel emotionally disconnected or dissatisfied within their primary relationships.

However, it is important to recognize that the virtual world is not a substitute for real-life connections and that the consequences of online infidelity can be significant. The impact of cyber infidelity extends beyond the digital realm and can profoundly affect individuals, relationships, and families.

Cyber infidelity and its impact on relationships

Cyber infidelity refers to the engagement in secretive and intimate interactions with someone other than one's committed partner through digital means. It can take various forms, including online flirting, sexting, emotional connections, or engaging in explicit content consumption.

The impact of cyber infidelity on relationships can be devastating. It erodes trust, creates emotional distance, and can lead to the breakdown of communication and intimacy. The secretive nature of cyber infidelity further compounds the pain and betrayal experienced by the partner who discovers the online involvement.

Addressing the impact of cyber infidelity requires open communication, transparency, and a commitment to rebuilding trust. It may involve setting clear boundaries regarding online behaviors, seeking professional support, and developing strategies for digital well-being within the relationship.

Conclusion

The internet has revolutionized the way we connect and form relationships, but it has also introduced new challenges and complexities in the realm of infidelity. Online dating platforms and affair websites provide individuals with convenient access to potential partners, while the allure of virtual connections and the anonymity factor can fuel the temptation to seek extramarital connections.

Understanding the dynamics of the internet and infidelity is crucial for individuals to navigate the digital landscape responsibly and ethically. It requires awareness of the motivations behind seeking online connections, recognizing the risks and consequences associated with cyber infidelity, and taking proactive steps towards healthy relationship fulfillment.

As we progress through the subsequent chapters of "Beyond Betrayal: Understanding and Healing from Infidelity," we will continue to explore healing processes, prevention strategies, and the exploration of emotional affair dynamics, incorporating the insights gained from understanding the complexities of the internet and infidelity.

Introduction

Infidelity is not limited to physical encounters alone. Emotional affairs, which involve developing intense emotional connections outside of one's committed partnership, can be just as damaging and painful. In this chapter of "Beyond Betrayal: Understanding and Healing from Infidelity," we explore the intricate dynamics of emotional affairs. We examine how friendships can evolve into emotional infidelity, the formation of deep emotional bonds, the impact of betrayals within these connections, and the importance of emotional fidelity within committed relationships. By understanding these dynamics, individuals can navigate the complexities of emotional affairs and work towards healing and strengthening their relationships.

Friendship turning into emotional infidelity

Emotional affairs often originate from seemingly innocent friendships that gradually evolve into something more intimate and emotionally charged. These connections may develop through shared interests, common experiences, or a deep emotional connection that goes beyond what is considered appropriate within the boundaries of a committed relationship.

What distinguishes emotional affairs from platonic friendships is the level of emotional investment and secrecy involved. Individuals engaged in emotional affairs may confide in their "friend" about personal matters, seek emotional support, or experience a sense of emotional connection that is lacking in their primary partnership.

It is essential to recognize the potential risks and boundaries that can be crossed when friendships blur into emotional infidelity. Maintaining open communication and transparency within committed relationships can help prevent the erosion of emotional fidelity.

Emotional bonds and betrayals

Emotional affairs are characterized by the formation of deep emotional bonds between individuals involved. These bonds can be intense, intimate, and may involve sharing vulnerable aspects of one's life. Emotional connections in affairs can provide a sense of understanding, validation, and emotional fulfillment that may be absent within the primary relationship.

However, when emotional affairs are discovered, the impact of the betrayal can be devastating. The sense of betrayal arises from the emotional investment and the perceived breach of trust. The hurt partner may experience a range of emotions, including anger, sadness, and a loss of trust in both the partner and themselves.

Understanding the dynamics of emotional bonds and the potential for betrayals can help individuals navigate these complex situations with empathy and compassion. It requires honest self-reflection, a willingness to address underlying relationship issues, and a commitment to rebuilding trust and emotional connection.

The importance of emotional fidelity

Emotional fidelity is an essential aspect of committed relationships. It encompasses being emotionally present, supportive, and engaged with one's partner. Emotional fidelity means actively nurturing the emotional connection within the relationship and recognizing the boundaries of emotional intimacy with others.

Emotional fidelity goes beyond physical exclusivity and highlights the importance of emotional transparency and vulnerability. It involves prioritizing the emotional well-being of one's partner and cultivating a deep sense of emotional trust and security.

Recognizing the significance of emotional fidelity can help individuals safeguard their relationships against emotional affairs. It requires ongoing communication, a commitment to open dialogue, and a willingness to address emotional needs and concerns within the partnership.

Conclusion

Emotional affairs bring a unique set of challenges and complexities to the realm of infidelity. The transformation of friendships into emotional infidelity, the formation of deep emotional bonds, the impact of betrayals, and the importance of emotional fidelity within committed relationships all contribute to the intricate dynamics of emotional affairs.

Understanding these dynamics is crucial for individuals to navigate the challenges of emotional affairs and work towards healing and strengthening their relationships. It requires open communication, empathy, and a commitment to emotional transparency and vulnerability.

As we progress through the subsequent chapters of "Beyond Betrayal: Understanding and Healing from Infidelity," we will continue to explore healing processes, prevention strategies, and the exploration of discovering the affair and its impact, incorporating the insights gained from understanding the complexities of emotional affair dynamics.

Chapter 12. Discovering the Affair: Impact and Trauma

Introduction

Discovering that your partner has engaged in an affair is a deeply distressing and life-altering experience. In this chapter of "Beyond Betrayal: Understanding and Healing from Infidelity," we delve into the profound impact and trauma that accompanies the discovery of an affair. We explore the emotional and psychological responses to betrayal, the complexities of confrontation and disclosure, the aftermath of the revelation, and coping strategies for the hurt partner. By understanding and acknowledging these aspects, individuals can begin the healing process and work towards rebuilding their lives and relationships.

Emotional and psychological responses to betrayal

The discovery of an affair can trigger a wide range of emotional and psychological responses for the hurt partner. Shock, disbelief, anger, sadness, and intense emotional pain are common reactions. Betrayal shatters the foundation of trust and security within the relationship, leaving the hurt partner questioning their self-worth and the authenticity of the entire relationship.

The emotional and psychological impact of betrayal can lead to a range of symptoms, such as anxiety, depression, loss of self-esteem, and difficulties in trusting others. The hurt partner may experience intrusive thoughts and images related to the affair, leading to a constant state of emotional turmoil.

Confrontation, disclosure, and aftermath

Confronting the unfaithful partner about the affair and seeking disclosure can be an emotionally charged and challenging process. The hurt partner often grapples with the fear of further deception or minimizing of the betrayal. However, open and honest communication is crucial for understanding the extent of the affair, its underlying causes, and the potential for healing and reconciliation.

Following the confrontation and disclosure, both partners must navigate the aftermath of the revelation. This stage involves a complex mix of emotions, including grief, anger, and confusion. The hurt partner may oscillate between wanting to salvage the relationship and contemplating ending it entirely.

Coping strategies for the hurt partner

Coping with the impact of an affair requires considerable emotional resilience and support. The hurt partner can adopt various coping strategies to navigate the tumultuous journey of healing:

Seeking professional support: Engaging in individual therapy or couples counseling can provide a safe space to process emotions, gain insight, and develop coping mechanisms.

Practicing self-care: Prioritizing self-care activities, such as exercise, relaxation techniques, and engaging in hobbies, can promote emotional well-being and aid in the healing process.

Establishing boundaries: Setting clear boundaries regarding communication, contact with the affair partner, and expectations within the relationship is essential for regaining a sense of safety and rebuilding trust.

Engaging in self-reflection: **Reflecting on personal values, needs, and desires can contribute to personal growth and assist in making informed decisions about the future of the relationship.**

Building a support network: **Seeking support from trusted friends, family members, or support groups can provide validation, understanding, and a sense of community during the healing process.**

Conclusion

Discovering an affair is a devastating experience that has a profound impact on the hurt partner's emotional and psychological well-being. Understanding and acknowledging the emotional and psychological responses to betrayal, navigating the complexities of confrontation and disclosure, and adopting effective coping strategies are essential steps towards healing and rebuilding.

As we progress through the subsequent chapters of "Beyond Betrayal: Understanding and Healing from Infidelity," we will continue to explore the intricacies of repairing the relationship, consequences and repercussions, and cultural responses to infidelity. Incorporating the insights gained from understanding the impact and trauma of discovering an affair, we can provide individuals with the necessary tools and support to move forward on their journey of healing and growth.

Introduction

After the devastating revelation of an affair, many couples find themselves grappling with the question: Can the relationship be repaired? In this chapter of "Beyond Betrayal: Understanding and Healing from Infidelity," we explore the possibility of rebuilding trust and healing the wounds inflicted by infidelity. We delve into the role of therapy and professional guidance in the process, as well as the factors that contribute to successful reconciliation. By understanding these dynamics, individuals can make informed decisions about the future of their relationship and embark on a path towards healing and restoration.

The possibility of rebuilding trust after an affair

Rebuilding trust after an affair is undoubtedly a challenging endeavor. Trust, once shattered, takes time, effort, and consistent actions to rebuild. The hurt partner must confront feelings of betrayal, vulnerability, and fear of future infidelity. The unfaithful partner, on the other hand, must demonstrate remorse, transparency, and a genuine commitment to change.

Rebuilding trust requires open and honest communication, active listening, and a willingness to address the underlying issues that contributed to the affair. It involves the establishment of new boundaries, increased accountability, and a shared commitment to the restoration of the relationship.

The role of therapy and professional guidance

Seeking therapy and professional guidance can be instrumental in the healing process after an affair. Couples therapy provides a safe and structured environment for both partners to explore their emotions, improve communication skills, and gain insights into the underlying dynamics that contributed to the infidelity.

Therapy offers an opportunity to address unresolved issues, develop coping strategies, and work towards rebuilding trust. A skilled therapist can guide the couple through the complex emotional terrain, facilitate productive discussions, and provide tools for effective conflict resolution and intimacy-building.

Individual therapy can also be beneficial, as it allows each partner to address personal healing, process individual emotions, and work on self-improvement. Healing individually contributes to the overall healing of the relationship.

Factors contributing to successful reconciliation

Successful reconciliation after infidelity depends on various factors. These include:

Genuine remorse and accountability: The unfaithful partner must take responsibility for their actions, express genuine remorse, and demonstrate a commitment to change. This includes being transparent, accountable, and making amends for the hurt caused.

Open and honest communication: Rebuilding trust requires open and honest communication. Both partners must be willing to listen, validate each other's feelings, and express their needs and concerns in a non-judgmental manner.

Patience and time: Healing and rebuilding trust take time. Both partners must be patient with the process, allowing for healing to occur at its own pace. Rushing or pressuring the hurt partner to move on too quickly can hinder the healing process.

Willingness to address underlying issues: Successful reconciliation involves addressing the underlying issues that contributed to the infidelity. This may include exploring relationship dynamics, communication patterns, unmet needs, and individual vulnerabilities.

Commitment to growth and change: Both partners must be committed to personal growth and making necessary changes to prevent future infidelity. This includes developing healthy coping mechanisms, improving communication skills, and cultivating a deeper understanding of each other's needs.

Conclusion

Repairing a relationship after infidelity is a challenging and complex journey, but it is possible with dedication, commitment, and a willingness to heal. Rebuilding trust requires time, effort, and professional guidance. By addressing the underlying issues, improving communication, and fostering a shared commitment to growth, couples can navigate the path towards healing and ultimately rebuild a stronger and more resilient relationship.

As we progress through the subsequent chapters of "Beyond Betrayal: Understanding and Healing from

Infidelity," we will continue to explore the consequences and repercussions of infidelity, cultural responses and perspectives, and strategies for preventing future betrayals. Incorporating the insights gained from understanding the process of repairing the relationship, individuals can move forward with hope, resilience, and the potential for a renewed connection.

Introduction

Infidelity is not limited to its immediate participants; its consequences ripple through the lives of all those involved. In this chapter of "Beyond Betrayal: Understanding and Healing from Infidelity," we delve into the far-reaching effects of infidelity, exploring the emotional and psychological impacts on both parties, the implications for children and extended family, as well as the legal aspects and potential consequences. By understanding these consequences and repercussions, individuals can gain insight into the breadth of the impact and work towards healing and resolution.

Emotional and psychological effects on both parties

Infidelity has profound emotional and psychological effects on both the unfaithful partner and the hurt partner. The unfaithful partner may experience guilt, shame, and a sense of moral conflict. They may grapple with self-doubt, regret, and the need to confront their actions and their impact on the relationship.

The hurt partner, on the other hand, often experiences a range of intense emotions such as anger, betrayal, sadness, and a loss of self-esteem. They may struggle with trust issues, persistent thoughts about the affair, and a sense of questioning their own worthiness and desirability.

Both partners may also face challenges in navigating their roles and identities within the relationship, as the power dynamics and emotional dynamics are significantly altered by the affair.

The impact on children and extended family

Infidelity has a significant impact on children and extended family members who may be indirectly affected by the betrayal. Children may experience confusion, anxiety, and a sense of instability within the family unit. The emotional well-being of children can be compromised, as they witness the aftermath of the affair and may be caught in the crossfire of their parents' emotions.

Extended family members, such as parents, siblings, and close friends, may also be impacted by the infidelity. They may feel torn between their loyalty to both parties, experience a sense of betrayal themselves, and struggle to navigate the complexities of maintaining relationships amidst the fallout.

Legal aspects and potential consequences

Infidelity can have legal implications, particularly in the context of divorce or separation. In some jurisdictions, infidelity can be grounds for divorce and may impact the division of assets, child custody arrangements, and spousal support determinations. It is important for individuals to consult with legal professionals to understand the specific legal implications in their jurisdiction and to navigate the legal process with clarity and guidance.

Additionally, infidelity can have broader social consequences, impacting one's reputation within their community, workplace, or social circles. These repercussions can vary depending on cultural norms, societal expectations, and the nature of the relationships involved.

Conclusion

Infidelity carries far-reaching consequences and repercussions that extend beyond the immediate participants. The emotional and psychological effects on both parties, the impact on children and extended family members, and the potential legal and social consequences highlight the gravity of infidelity.

As we progress through the subsequent chapters of "Beyond Betrayal: Understanding and Healing from Infidelity," we will continue to explore cultural responses and perspectives on infidelity, healing and moving forward after an affair, and strategies for preventing future betrayals. Incorporating the insights gained from understanding the consequences and repercussions, individuals can approach their healing journey with empathy, understanding, and a commitment to growth and restoration.

Introduction

Infidelity is a universal phenomenon that transcends cultural boundaries, yet different cultures and societies respond to it in unique ways. In this chapter of "Beyond Betrayal: Understanding and Healing from Infidelity," we delve into the cultural responses and perspectives on infidelity. We explore how different cultures approach infidelity, the influence of religious views and moral dilemmas, and the cross-cultural variations in forgiveness and reconciliation. By understanding these cultural nuances, individuals can gain insight into the diverse ways in which infidelity is perceived and navigate their own healing journey with a broader perspective.

How different cultures approach infidelity

Cultural attitudes towards infidelity vary significantly across different societies. Some cultures may view infidelity as a grave transgression, while others may have more permissive attitudes or alternative relationship structures that accommodate non-monogamous behaviors. Understanding these cultural perspectives helps contextualize the responses of individuals and communities to infidelity.

In some cultures, infidelity is strictly condemned and considered a breach of trust, leading to severe consequences such as divorce, social ostracization, or even violence. In contrast, other cultures may adopt a more tolerant or pragmatic approach, acknowledging that infidelity can occur within the context of long-term relationships and choosing to focus on the preservation of other aspects of the relationship.

Religious views and moral dilemmas

Religion plays a significant role in shaping cultural responses to infidelity. Different religious beliefs and moral frameworks provide guidance on fidelity, marriage, and sexual ethics. These religious views can influence individuals' attitudes towards infidelity and their sense of moral responsibility.

Religious teachings may emphasize the importance of marital commitment and fidelity, positioning infidelity as a betrayal of religious principles. However, religious communities also differ in their responses to infidelity, ranging from strict condemnations to offering forgiveness and opportunities for redemption.

Cross-cultural variations in forgiveness and reconciliation

Forgiveness and reconciliation are complex processes that vary across cultures. Cultural norms and values influence the propensity to forgive, the conditions for reconciliation, and the extent of social support provided to couples navigating the aftermath of infidelity.

In some cultures, forgiveness is viewed as a virtue and a means of restoring harmony within relationships and communities. These cultures may emphasize the importance of redemption, second chances, and the preservation of family unity. In contrast, other cultures may prioritize individual autonomy, self-preservation, or the public perception of maintaining dignity, leading to a lower inclination towards forgiveness and reconciliation.

Conclusion

Cultural responses and perspectives on infidelity shape individuals' understanding of betrayal and influence the available resources and support systems for healing. By recognizing the diverse approaches to infidelity, individuals can navigate their own healing journey with cultural sensitivity and open-mindedness. It is essential to acknowledge that there is no universally right or wrong response to infidelity and that cultural contexts play a significant role in shaping individual experiences and choices.

As we progress through the subsequent chapters of "Beyond Betrayal: Understanding and Healing from Infidelity," we will continue to explore healing and moving forward after an affair, strategies for preventing future betrayals, and redefining relationships beyond infidelity. Incorporating the insights gained from understanding cultural responses and perspectives, individuals can approach their healing journey with a greater appreciation for diversity and a more comprehensive understanding of the complexities surrounding infidelity.

Introduction

Recovering from the pain of infidelity is a challenging journey that requires intentional effort, support, and a commitment to healing. In this chapter of "Beyond Betrayal: Understanding and Healing from Infidelity," we explore the process of healing and moving forward after the devastation of betrayal. We delve into the importance of individual and couple's therapy for recovery, the essential steps in rebuilding self-esteem and trust, and the growth opportunities that can arise from the aftermath of an affair. By understanding these aspects, individuals can find the strength and resilience to move beyond the pain and discover a path towards healing and growth.

Individual and couple's therapy for recovery

Therapy plays a crucial role in the healing process after an affair. Individual therapy provides a safe and supportive space for the hurt partner to explore their emotions, address their trauma, and work towards personal healing and growth. A skilled therapist can guide the hurt partner through the complex emotions of grief, anger, and betrayal, helping them develop coping strategies, rebuild self-esteem, and regain a sense of identity.

Couple's therapy is equally important, as it offers an opportunity for both partners to come together and address the underlying issues that contributed to the infidelity. In therapy, couples can learn effective communication skills, develop empathy and understanding, and work towards rebuilding trust and intimacy. A therapist can help facilitate productive conversations, guide the couple through forgiveness and reconciliation processes, and provide tools for long-term relationship success.

Rebuilding self-esteem and trust

The aftermath of infidelity often leaves the hurt partner with shattered self-esteem and a deep sense of betrayal. Rebuilding self-esteem is a critical step towards healing and moving forward. It involves recognizing one's worth, embracing self-care practices, and engaging in activities that bring joy and fulfillment. Through therapy, individuals can challenge negative self-perceptions, develop self-compassion, and cultivate a positive sense of self.

Rebuilding trust is a gradual process that requires consistent effort and open communication. The unfaithful partner must demonstrate transparency, accountability, and a commitment to change. They need to understand the impact of their actions, validate the hurt partner's emotions, and take responsibility for rebuilding trust. The hurt partner, on the other hand, must be willing to forgive and work towards trust restoration, while setting boundaries and engaging in open and honest dialogue.

Growth opportunities after an affair

Although infidelity is a deeply painful experience, it can also provide opportunities for growth and transformation. The crisis of betrayal often prompts individuals to reevaluate their values, priorities, and relationship dynamics. It can be an impetus for personal growth, as individuals learn to navigate their emotions, develop resilience, and build a stronger sense of self.

Couples who choose to work through the aftermath of infidelity may find that their relationship deepens and evolves. The process of rebuilding trust and addressing underlying issues can lead to a more authentic and intimate connection. It can also foster a renewed commitment to open communication, vulnerability, and shared growth.

Conclusion

Healing and moving forward after infidelity is a challenging but transformative journey. Through individual and couple's therapy, individuals can address their emotional wounds, rebuild self-esteem, and work towards trust restoration. Embracing growth opportunities and using the crisis of betrayal as a catalyst for personal and relational transformation can lead to a stronger, more resilient, and more fulfilling life beyond the pain of infidelity.

As we progress through the subsequent chapters of "Beyond Betrayal: Understanding and Healing from Infidelity," we will continue to explore strategies for preventing future betrayals, the importance of nurturing healthy relationships, and redefining relationships beyond infidelity. Incorporating the insights gained from understanding the healing process, individuals can approach their journey with hope, resilience, and the belief that there is life and love beyond betrayal.

Introduction

While healing and recovery from infidelity are crucial aspects of overcoming betrayal, prevention is equally important. In this chapter of "Beyond Betrayal: Understanding and Healing from Infidelity," we explore strategies for preventing infidelity, focusing on nurturing healthy relationships, fostering effective communication, strengthening emotional bonds and intimacy, and developing proactive measures to safeguard commitment. By understanding these preventive measures, individuals can cultivate resilient relationships and reduce the likelihood of experiencing the pain and devastation of betrayal.

Nurturing healthy relationships and effective communication

The foundation of preventing infidelity lies in nurturing healthy relationships and establishing effective communication patterns. Healthy relationships are built on trust, respect, and open dialogue. Partners should prioritize spending quality time together, engaging in shared activities, and cultivating a deep emotional connection. By actively investing in the relationship, partners can build a strong bond that helps protect against the temptation of infidelity.

Effective communication is vital in preventing misunderstandings and addressing potential issues before they escalate. Partners should cultivate active listening skills, express their needs and concerns openly and honestly, and create a safe space for vulnerability and emotional expression. Clear and open communication helps maintain transparency, understanding, and mutual support, reducing the likelihood of unmet needs and emotional disconnection that may lead to infidelity.

Strengthening emotional bonds and intimacy

Emotional intimacy is a key component of a strong and resilient relationship. Partners should strive to deepen their emotional connection by expressing love, appreciation, and gratitude for each other. Engaging in meaningful conversations, sharing hopes and dreams, and providing emotional support during challenging times strengthens the bond between partners and fosters a sense of security and closeness.

Additionally, cultivating a fulfilling and satisfying sexual relationship is essential. Partners should prioritize sexual intimacy and explore ways to enhance their sexual connection. Open and honest communication about desires, needs, and boundaries can promote a healthy sexual relationship and reduce the risk of seeking fulfillment outside the partnership.

Developing strategies to prevent infidelity

Proactive measures can be taken to protect a relationship from the threat of infidelity. Partners should establish clear boundaries and expectations, discussing what is acceptable behavior within the relationship and what constitutes a breach of trust. Boundaries may include guidelines for interactions with individuals outside the relationship, such as colleagues or friends of the opposite sex.

Cultivating a strong support system is also crucial. Maintaining healthy friendships and social connections outside the relationship provides individuals with emotional support, outlets for personal growth, and opportunities for fulfillment. Having a supportive network reduces the likelihood of seeking emotional or physical intimacy elsewhere.

Regularly reassessing the relationship and addressing potential issues promptly is another preventive measure. Partners should engage in ongoing conversations about their needs, desires, and overall relationship satisfaction. By addressing concerns early on, couples can work together to find resolutions and maintain a strong connection.

Conclusion

Preventing infidelity requires a proactive and ongoing commitment to building and safeguarding a healthy relationship. Nurturing healthy relationships, fostering effective communication, strengthening emotional bonds and intimacy, and developing strategies to protect against the temptation of infidelity are essential steps. By taking these preventive measures, individuals can create a relationship built on trust, connection, and commitment, reducing the likelihood of experiencing the pain and aftermath of betrayal.

As we progress through the subsequent chapters of "Beyond Betrayal: Understanding and Healing from Infidelity," we will continue to explore the importance of effective communication, redefining relationships, and understanding evolving relationship models. Incorporating the insights gained from understanding prevention strategies, individuals can approach their relationships with a proactive mindset, fostering a love that is resilient, fulfilling, and faithful.

Introduction

Infidelity can shake the foundations of a relationship, prompting individuals to question traditional notions of monogamy and explore alternative relationship models. In this chapter of "Beyond Betrayal: Understanding and Healing from Infidelity," we delve into the concept of redefining relationships beyond infidelity. We explore open relationships, consensual non-monogamy, alternatives to traditional monogamy, and the evolving landscape of relationship models. By examining these possibilities, individuals can navigate their own paths and find a relationship structure that aligns with their values, needs, and desires.

Open relationships and consensual non-monogamy

Open relationships and consensual non-monogamy are relationship structures where partners agree to engage in romantic or sexual relationships with multiple people while maintaining a primary partnership. These alternative relationship models challenge the traditional notion of exclusivity and offer the opportunity for honest exploration, personal growth, and emotional connection outside the primary relationship.

In open relationships, partners establish clear boundaries and guidelines for engaging with others. Communication, trust, and consent are vital components of this relationship structure. Open relationships can provide a sense of freedom, allowing individuals to meet their diverse emotional and sexual needs while maintaining a committed bond with their primary partner.

Alternatives to traditional monogamy

Beyond open relationships, individuals may explore other alternatives to traditional monogamy. These alternatives include polyamory, where individuals have multiple loving and committed relationships simultaneously, and relationship anarchy, which rejects societal expectations and allows individuals to shape their relationships based on individual desires and connections.

Polyamory emphasizes emotional connections and encourages individuals to develop meaningful relationships with multiple partners. It challenges the notion that love is a finite resource and celebrates the capacity for individuals to deeply love more than one person.

Relationship anarchy, on the other hand, emphasizes personal autonomy and freedom in relationships. It encourages individuals to navigate their connections organically, without predefined roles or expectations. Relationship anarchy promotes fluidity, allowing relationships to evolve and change naturally without societal norms dictating their form or trajectory.

Exploring evolving relationship models

The landscape of relationships is continually evolving, with individuals seeking relationship structures that align with their values and desires. Beyond open relationships, consensual non-monogamy, polyamory, and relationship anarchy, individuals may explore various relationship models such as long-distance relationships, living apart together (LAT) arrangements, or even non-romantic intimate partnerships.

Long-distance relationships require individuals to maintain emotional connection and commitment despite physical distance. Communication, trust, and shared goals are vital to the success of these relationships.

LAT arrangements allow individuals to maintain separate living spaces while being in a committed partnership. This arrangement offers individuals the opportunity to have personal space and independence while nurturing their relationship.

Non-romantic intimate partnerships challenge the traditional notion that romantic and sexual relationships are the only valid forms of intimate connections. These partnerships prioritize emotional support, companionship, and shared life goals without a romantic or sexual component.

Conclusion

Infidelity can prompt individuals to question traditional relationship structures and explore new possibilities. Open relationships, consensual non-monogamy, alternatives to traditional monogamy, and evolving relationship models offer individuals the opportunity to create relationships that are authentic, fulfilling, and aligned with their values and desires.

As we conclude this chapter of "Beyond Betrayal: Understanding and Healing from Infidelity," it is essential to recognize that there is no one-size-fits-all approach to relationships. Each individual and couple must navigate their own path, considering their unique circumstances and aspirations. By embracing the concept of redefining relationships, individuals can find a relationship structure that fosters growth, connection, and personal fulfillment, transcending the pain of infidelity and creating a future filled with love and authenticity.

"Beyond Betrayal: Understanding and Healing from Infidelity" delves deep into the intricate world of infidelity, offering a comprehensive exploration of its causes, consequences, and the path to healing.

Through eighteen thought-provoking chapters, this book navigates the complexities of infidelity, examining its various types, societal and cultural influences, psychological motivations, and the dynamics of communication and relationships that contribute to its occurrence.

From the impact of the internet and gender perspectives to the discovery of affairs and the potential for repairing relationships, this book offers insights, coping strategies, and a roadmap for rebuilding trust, growth, and ultimately redefining relationships beyond infidelity. It is a guidebook for those seeking understanding, healing, and the possibility of a brighter future.

ABOUT THE AUTHOR

Mr. C. P. Kumar is a retired Scientist 'G' from National Institute of Hydrology, Roorkee, Uttarakhand, India. He is also a Reiki Healer and Chakra Balancing practitioner (with pendulum dowsing) and offers Emotional Freedom Technique (EFT) to help individuals with emotional issues. Mr. Kumar has authored many books on technical, spiritual, and social topics.

For further details, you may visit his webpage
https://www.angelfire.com/nh/cpkumar/virgo.html

www.ingramcontent.com/pod-product-compliance
Lightning Source LLC
Chambersburg PA
CBHW052221150726

48002CB00003B/1212